THE WOMAN WHO INVENTED THE THREAD THAT STOPS BULLETS

The Genius of Stephanie Kwolek

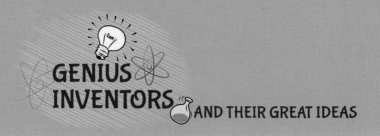

Titles in the *Genius Inventors and Their Great Ideas* Series:

The Man Who Invented the Ferris Wheel: The Genius of George Ferris
Library Ed. ISBN: 978-0-7660-4136-3
Paperback ISBN: 978-1-4644-0206-7 • EPUB ISBN: 978-1-4645-1119-6
Single-User PDF ISBN: 978-1-4646-1119-3 • Multi-User PDF ISBN: 978-0-7660-5748-7

The Man Who Invented the Electric Guitar: The Genius of Les Paul
Library Ed. ISBN: 978-0-7660-4137-0
Paperback ISBN: 978-1-4644-0207-4 • EPUB ISBN: 978-1-4645-1120-2
Single-User PDF ISBN: 978-1-4646-1120-9 • Multi-User PDF ISBN: 978-0-7660-5749-4

The Man Who Invented the Laser: The Genius of Theodore H. Maiman
Library Ed. ISBN: 978-0-7660-4138-7
Paperback ISBN: 978-1-4644-0208-1 • EPUB ISBN: 978-1-4645-1121-9
Single-User PDF ISBN: 978-1-4646-1121-6 • Multi-User PDF ISBN: 978-0-7660-5750-0

The Man Who Invented Television: The Genius of Philo T. Farnsworth
Library Ed. ISBN: 978-0-7660-4139-4
Paperback ISBN: 978-1-4644-0209-8 • EPUB ISBN: 978-1-4645-1122-6
Single-User PDF ISBN: 978-1-4646-1122-3 • Multi-User PDF ISBN: 978-0-7660-5751-7

The Woman Who Invented the Thread That Stops Bullets: The Genius of Stephanie Kwolek
Library Ed. ISBN: 978-0-7660-4141-7
Paperback ISBN: 978-1-4644-0211-1 • EPUB ISBN: 978-1-4645-1124-0
Single-User PDF ISBN: 978-1-4646-1124-7 • Multi-User PDF ISBN: 978-0-7660-5753-1

The Man Who Invented the Game of Basketball: The Genius of James Naismith
Library Ed. ISBN: 978-0-7660-4142-4
Paperback ISBN: 978-1-4644-0212-8 • EPUB ISBN: 978-1-4645-1125-7
Single-User PDF ISBN: 978-1-4646-1125-4 • Multi-User PDF ISBN: 978-0-7660-5754-8

GENIUS INVENTORS AND THEIR GREAT IDEAS

THE WOMAN WHO INVENTED THE THREAD THAT STOPS BULLETS

The Genius of Stephanie Kwolek

By Edwin Brit Wyckoff

Enslow Elementary

an imprint of

Enslow Publishers, Inc.

40 Industrial Road
Box 398
Berkeley Heights, NJ 07922
USA

http://www.enslow.com

Content Advisor
Nick Thomas, Ph.D
Chemistry Professor
Auburn University at Montgomery, Alabama

Series Literacy Consultant
Allan A. De Fina, Ph.D.
Past President of the New Jersey Reading Association
Chairperson, Derpartment of Literacy Education
New Jersey City University

Enslow Elementary, an imprint of Enslow Publishers, Inc.
Enslow Elementary® is a registered trademark of Enslow Publishers, Inc.

Original edition published as *Stopping Bullets with a Thread: Stephanie Kwolek and Her Incredible Invention* in 2008.

Library of Congress Cataloging-in-Publication Data

Wyckoff, Edwin Brit.
  The woman who invented the thread that stops bullets : the genius of Stephanie Kwolek / by Edwin Brit Wyckoff.
    p. cm. — (Genius inventors and their great ideas)
  Previously published: 2008.
  Includes bibliographical references and index.
    ISBN 978-0-7660-4141-7 (alk. paper)
  1. Kwolek, Stephanie, 1923—Juvenile literature. 2. Industrial chemists—United States—Biography—Juvenile literature. 3. Inventors—United States—Biography—Juvenile literature. 4. Ballistic fabrics—Juvenile literature. 5. Polyphenyleneterephthalamide—Juvenile literature. I. Title.
  TS1440.K96W93 2013
  660.092—dc23
  [B]
                                                    2012013980

Future editions:
Paperback ISBN: 978-1-4644-0211-1
Single-User PDF ISBN: 978-0-7660-1124-7

EPUB ISBN: 978-1-4645-1124-0
Multi-User PDF ISBN: 978-0-7660-5753-1

Printed in the United States of America.
032013 Lake Book Manufacturing, Inc., Melrose Park, IL
10 9 8 7 6 5 4 3 2 1

To Our Readers: We have done our best to make sure all Internet addresses in this book were active and appropriate when we went to press. However, the author and the publisher have no control over and assume no liability for the material available on those Internet sites or on other Web sites they may link to. Any comments or suggestions can be sent by e-mail to comments@enslow.com or to the address on the back cover.

♻ Enslow Publishers, Inc., is committed to printing our books on recycled paper. The paper in every book contains 10% to 30% post-consumer waste (PCW). The cover board on the outside of each book contains 100% PCW. Our goal is to do our part to help young people and the environment too!

Photo Credits: Alfred Pasieka/Photo Researchers, Inc., p. 24; Artville, p. 9; Charles D. Winters/Photo Researchers, Inc., p. 23; Courtesy of Carnegie Mellon University Archives, p. 16; Courtesy Daryl Wilson/Tulsa World, p.32; Courtesy Dupont, pp. 3, 5, 26, 29, 31; Courtesy Smithsonian Institute, with permission from Stephanie Kwolek, pp. 8, 13, 15 (right), 34; ©iStockphoto.com/Dieter Spears, p. 6; Library of Congress, Prints and Photographs, p. 17; Photos.com, p. 26; ©SCPhotos/Alamy, p. 27; Shane Anderson, p.11 (top); Shutterstock.com, pp. 11 (bottom), 14, 15 (left), 20, 22, 35, 39, 41, 42, 47; Susumu Nishinaga/Photo Researchers, Inc., p. 21; U.S. Marine Corps photo by Lance Cpl. Andres J. Lugo/Released, p. 33; William J. Clinton Presidential Library, p. 36.

Cover Photo: Stephanie Kwolek: Courtesy Dupont (color-enhanced), Soldier: Shutterstock.com

CONTENTS

This officer wears a vest like the one that saved Robert Miklich's life.

Chapter 1

The Deadliest Chase

A car went speeding through red light after red light on a highway in Pennsylvania. A state trooper's cruiser followed so closely it seemed that both cars were attached. With his siren screaming, Trooper Robert Miklich stomped on the gas pedal, trying to get ahead of the crazed driver he was chasing. Both cars skidded and darted through traffic. Finally the runaway car flew off the road and smashed into a bank of earth.

The driver threw open his door and ran into a field, trying to escape. Miklich ran after him. The suspect turned and shot Officer Miklich in his left shoulder. Blood poured from the policeman's shoulder. Another bullet hit him square in the chest, right over his heart. It was like being hit

Stephanie, here three years old, spent much time around animals when she was young.

by a sledgehammer. But there was no blood. There was no hole in Miklich's vest. His life had been saved by threads. He handcuffed the man with the gun and took him to jail. It seemed as though Superman had landed in Pennsylvania. But this wasn't fiction. It was real life.

The genius who invented the threads that saved Miklich's life was a quiet woman who had dreamed of becoming a doctor. She never did.

New Kensington, PA

Stephanie grew up in Pennsylvania.

Stephanie Kwolek was born on July 31, 1923, in New Kensington, Pennsylvania. As a young girl she knew how to walk quietly in the woods. Even the tiniest frog would not jump away from her. A snake would glide by. The girl was not scared by animals. She would not make a sound.

Stephanie's father, John, had taught her to see and remember. Together, they watched spiders build webs. They found paw prints in muddy puddles. Their secret outdoor world always changed. She collected leaves and seeds and skins the snakes would shed each spring. She pressed her treasures between the pages of her scrapbooks.

When she was ten, her father died. He had given her the gift of patience stronger than steel. He had taught her to remember what she had seen and heard. Someday that would turn her into a famous scientist. She never expected that, but it happened.

Stephanie and her father enjoyed the outdoor world.

Chapter 2

Designing Fashions and Fibers

America was going through hard times during the 1930s. People called it the Great Depression. Factories closed down. Men lost their jobs. Her mother, Nellie, found it almost impossible to get a job. Money was scarce. After a long search Nellie found a job working at the aluminum company in town.

Because of her mother's job, Stephanie had to take care of her younger brother every day after school.

Ten-year-old Stephanie took care of her brother, who was two years younger, after school.

She also spent time alone designing beautiful clothes. Her dresses looked as good as the pictures in fashion magazines. All through grade school she sewed clothing tiny enough to fit her dolls. Each stitch had to be perfect. Stephanie began to dream about becoming a famous dress designer. One of her happiest dreams was to one day show off her beautiful clothes on elegant models in Paris, France. Her designs would cost a lot of money. Everybody would buy them. Everybody would wear them.

Stephanie liked to sew dresses for her dolls. She wanted to be a fashion designer when she grew up.

High school was an exciting new world for Stephanie. The chemistry laboratory fascinated her. It had shiny glass test tubes. Clear beakers were filled with bright, beautiful, colored chemicals. She learned how to measure and mix chemicals very carefully. She heated them over a laboratory burner. The chemicals boiled and bubbled. Different things happened. She took careful notes. That made her think of her father. He had taught her to watch and remember what happened.

Shifting from perfect sewing to precise chemistry experiments was a natural step for Stephanie. The good chemist in her became better and better. Her next step was to become a doctor. Dreams like that cost money her family did not have. Stephanie decided to major in chemistry at college. She planned on saving up money working as a chemist. Later on, she could go to medical school. The Carnegie Institute of Technology in Pittsburgh, Pennsylvania, was a good place to study chemistry. She entered that college in 1942.

Stephanie enjoyed her high school chemistry classes.

Stephanie attended the all-girls college at the Carnegie Institute of Technology in Pittsburgh, Pennsylvania.

The country was fighting World War II. Millions of men went to war overseas. Companies were eager to hire women as chemists, engineers, and almost anything else. But when Kwolek graduated in 1946, the war was over.

This woman helped build airplanes during World War II. After the war, it was harder for women to find jobs.

Soldiers were coming home looking for jobs. Women began finding it hard to get work they had trained for. That was not fair.

Kwolek went to see DuPont, a company in Buffalo, New York. They did not offer her a job until she was able to persuade them that she loved chemistry. DuPont gave her a job searching for new ways to make thread and cloth out of chemicals. Kwolek moved to Buffalo. She would stay with DuPont for forty years, running thousands of experiments.

Chapter 3

Challenging Nature

Nature has always made wonderful fibers such as cotton, wool, and silk. The fibers can be turned into thread that is woven into cloth. Cotton, which grows on plants, is made into shirts, sheets, towels, and all kinds of clothing. Wool is clipped from sheep. It is made into blankets and warm clothing. Silk worms spin out miles of silk fibers that make neckties, scarves, and expensive clothes people love. Nature is hard to beat.

Kwolek and the other chemists in the laboratory knew that fibers like nylon were made from chemicals found in coal, petroleum, and natural gas. Nobody had to plant fields of cotton. Nobody had to raise herds of sheep to gather wool. Chemicals were mixed together to make fibers

Natural fibers include cotton from the cotton plant, wool from sheep, and silk from silkworms.

called synthetics. They were designed to be cheaper, stronger, or warmer than nature could make. Finding the right mixture of chemicals can take years and years.

Kwolek searched for new fibers by taking chemicals from petroleum, which comes from deep underground. Usually it is made into gasoline for cars or turned into all kinds of plastics. Her job was to create the stiffest, strongest fibers ever made. They could be used to replace the steel built into the sides of automobile tires.

Her team of chemists produced thousands of liquid fibers. Then they spun the liquid fibers into thread. Spinning means pushing the chemical fibers through tiny holes in a steel plate. Threads come out the other side. None of the experiments produced anything as stiff or as strong as steel.

This close-up view of man-made fibers shows how they can be woven together.

Many chemists in the laboratory gave up on the project. But Kwolek's father had taught her patience. She kept on testing and studying. When the company built a big, more modern laboratory in Wilmington, Delaware, Kwolek moved there in 1950.

Wells pump petroleum out of the earth.

Liquid fibers, like nylon, can be spun into thread.

POLYMERS

Polymers are chains of chemicals attached to each other. They are made by nature and by scientists. This is a typical polymer.

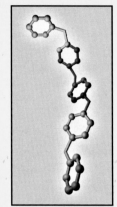

This is a computer drawing of a polymer chain.

Kwolek never gave up. More than one hundred thousand long chains of chemicals called polymers were developed and tested. Her work went on for more than ten years. Most of the experiments produced beautiful, clear liquids that flowed slowly like molasses. Some of them were spun into threads. Not one of the threads was stiff enough or strong enough to replace steel.

Chapter 4

The Cloudy Outlook

"I made a discovery," Kwolek told a reporter. A batch of liquid chemicals looked cloudy and was as thin as water. She looked at it through a microscope. The parts of the chemical chains were straight sticks "like spaghetti lined up next to each other," she said. "Anyone who wasn't thinking would have thrown it out," she added. Kwolek did not throw it out. Her father had taught her to stop and think.

Kwolek sent a batch of this cloudy mixture to the spinning room. She wanted it spun into threads. "The guy in charge of spinning refused to spin the liquid," she remembers. He told her it would gum up his machines. Kwolek was a gentle person. But she never liked the word *no.*

Kwolek used her microscope to see the spaghetti-like fibers in her batch of cloudy liquid.

Kevlar thread has a golden color.

The man said *no* again and again. Kwolek said *please*. She said it nicely. She said it every day. "Either I wore him down or he felt sorry for me," she said, laughing, as she remembered the day the spinning began.

Something strange happened during the spinning. The links in the chain that looked like spaghetti lined up next to each other. Kwolek sent the thread to the testing department. They reported that it was nine times stiffer than any thread ever invented. The cloudy stuff was clearly five times stronger than steel.

The United States Patent Office granted Kwolek and her supervisor, Paul Morgan, a patent for the fiber in 1966. A patent is just a piece of paper, but it protects the inventors. It was legal proof Kwolek and Morgan had invented the fiber that, later on, would be called Kevlar®.

There is still a giant step from tiny lab experiments to making huge batches in a factory. DuPont chemists worked five more years and spent 400 million dollars learning how to make cloth that could stop bullets. They struggled to manufacture rope strong enough to pull a locomotive. In 1971, the first product made of Kevlar went on the market. Since then, more than two hundred products have depended on the unbelievable strength and stiffness of Stephanie Kwolek's invention.

The material Kwolek discovered was so strong that needles testing it would bend rather than pierce through it.

Chapter 5

The Survivors' Club

Kevlar can be the difference between life and death. More than three thousand police and corrections officers are alive today because of body armor made with Kwolek's Kevlar. It helped them survive being shot, stabbed, dragged, and other dangers.

A policeman on a motorcycle in Oklahoma chased a car that roared by at about ninety miles an hour. His siren blasted a warning. He flicked his headlight a dozen times and got so close he could see the driver's eyes in the car's rearview mirror. All of a sudden the car became a weapon. The driver slammed on his brakes so hard the tires left 188 feet of black rubber marks on the road. Officer Ron Clark's cycle flipped on its side dragging him hundreds of

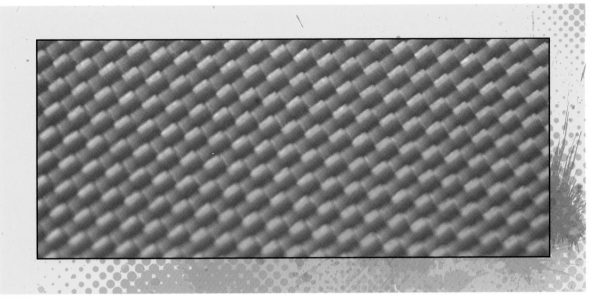

Threads of Kevlar can be woven into a fabric strong enough to stop bullets.

feet along the highway. The car sped off leaving the officer for dead. He was scraped, bruised, and bleeding heavily, but very much alive. Without body armor made from Kevlar he would have been lost.

Kevlar went to war in 1991. War is awful. It is not like a video game. Real bullets are shot at real soldiers. Even heavy steel armor may not save human lives. Since 1991 American and British soldiers have worn helmets made with Kevlar. Soldiers also wear body armor made with Kevlar to stop bullets and bombs.

"Not in a thousand years did I think the discovery of Kevlar would save thousands of lives," Stephanie Kwolek said. She was not thinking about war when she invented Kevlar. Her job was to think about stiffness and strength. Now there is a survivors' club of police officers. Some of them ask Ko Kwolek to sign their precious vests.

Officer Ron Clark's body armor made with Kevlar saved his life. His flipped motorcycle dragged him along U.S. Route 75 in Tulsa, Oklahoma.

In September 2006, Corporal Daniel Greenwald was shot in the head by a sniper in Iraq. Thanks to the Kevlar in his helmet, he escaped with only an inch-long cut in his forehead.

Young Stephanie wanted to save lives as a doctor. Instead, she grew up and learned to save lives as a chemist. Kwolek spoke from her heart when she said, "I feel very humble. I feel very lucky. So many people work all their

Kwolek holds a model of the Kevlar polymer.

THE MANY USES OF KEVLAR

Kevlar can be made into more than two hundred products. Here are a few examples:

- Bulletproof helmets for soldiers
- Body armor for police and soldiers
- Suspension cables for bridges
- Brake pads for cars
- Hiking and camping gear
- Sails
- Skis, skateboards, and snowboards
- Outer shells for spacecraft
- Safety helmets for work and sports
- Safety linings for jet engines
- Radial automobile tires
- Rope strong enough to pull a railroad engine

Kwolek received the National Medal of Technology from President Bill Clinton in 1996.

lives and they don't have a big break or make a discovery that's of benefit to other people."

She remembered her years of work. "I seem to see things other people did not see. If things don't work out, I struggle over them. You have to have an open mind," she recalled.

Kwolek retired to her home near the laboratory in Wilmington in 1986. The brilliant chemist never forgot her love of designing and sewing. She bought herself a new sewing machine.

Her name is on seventeen patents and all kinds of honorary awards. Kwolek still has that wonderful, wide-open mind. And, this above all, she still doesn't like no for an answer.

TIMELINE

1923—Born July 31 in New Kensington, Pennsylvania.

1933—Father dies; mother goes to work for aluminum company.

1942—Enters chemistry program at Carnegie Institute of Technology in Pittsburgh, Pennsylvania.

1946—Graduates with bachelor's degree in chemistry; lands a job with DuPont in Buffalo, New York.

1950—Moves to Wilmington, Dleaware, to work at DuPont's textile fibers laboratory.

1966—United States Patent Office grants patent for fibers later called Kevlar.

1971—Products made with Kevlar first marketed.

1986—Retires from Dupont.

1994—National Inventor's Hall of Fame honors her work.

1999—Earns Lemelson-MIT Lifetime Achievement Award.

2003—Becomes 185th member of the National Women's Hall of Fame.

YOU BE THE INVENTOR!

So you want to be an inventor? You can do it! First, you need a terrific idea.

Got a problem? No problem!

Many inventions begin when someone thinks of a great solution to a problem. One cold day in 1994, 10-year-old K.K. Gregory was building a snow fort. Soon, she had snow between her mittens and her coat sleeve. Her wrists were cold and wet. She found some scraps of fabric around the house, and used them to make a tube that would fit around her wrist. She cut a thumbhole in the tube to

make a kind of fingerless glove, and called it a "Wristie." Wearing mittens over her new invention, her wrists stayed nice and warm when she played outside. Today, the Wristie business is booming.

Now it's your turn. Maybe, like K.K. Gregory, you have an idea for something new that would make your life better or easier. Perhaps you can think of a way improve an everyday item. Twelve-year-old Becky Schroeder became the youngest female ever to receive a U.S. patent after she invented a glow-in-the-dark clipboard that allowed people to write in the dark. Do you like to play sports or board games? James Naismith, inspired by a game he used to play as a boy, invented a new game he called basketball.

Let your imagination run wild. You never know where it will take you.

Research it!

Okay, you have a terrific idea for an invention. Now what? First, you'll want to make sure that nobody else has thought of your idea. You wouldn't want to spend hours developing your new invention, only to find that someone else beat you to it. Google Patents can help you find out whether your idea is original.

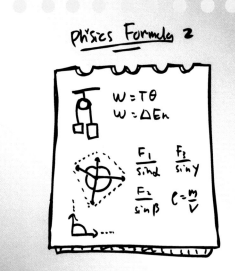

Bring it to life!

If no one else has thought of your idea, congratulations! Write it down in a logbook or journal. Write the date and your initials for every entry you make. If you file a patent for your invention later, this will help you prove that you were the first person to think of it. The most important thing about this logbook is that pages cannot be added or subtracted. You can buy a bound notebook at any office supply store.

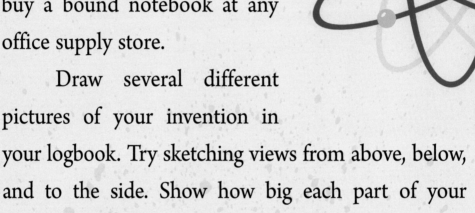

Draw several different pictures of your invention in your logbook. Try sketching views from above, below, and to the side. Show how big each part of your invention should be.

Build a model. Don't be discouraged if it doesn't work at first. You may have to experiment with different designs and materials. That's part of the fun! Take pictures of everything, and tape them into your logbook.

Try your invention out on your friends and family. If they have any suggestions to make it better, build another model. Perfect your invention, and give it a clever name.

Patent it!

Do you want to sell your invention? You'll want to apply for a patent. Holding a patent to your invention means that no one else can make, use, or sell your invention in the U.S. without your permission. It prevents others from making money off of your idea. You will definitely need an adult to help you apply for a patent. It can be a complicated and expensive process. But if you think that people will want to buy your invention, it is well worth it.

GLOSSARY

armor—Clothing made of steel to protect a person from swords, knives, or bullets.

chemistry—The study of how materials, like fabrics, metals, and plastics, are made and how they react with other materials.

experiment—A test of something never tried before.

fiber—A very thin material, like a short bit of hair from a sheep. Fibers can be spun into thread.

Great Depression—In 1929, many people in the United States became poor. They could not find jobs. This problem continued all through the 1930s and its effects were felt around the world.

molecule—The smallest part of anything. Steel, food, wood, and air are all made up of molecules.

polymer—A whole chain of the same molecule.

precise—Careful, perfect, absolutely accurate.

retire—To stop working after you have worked for many years.

sledgehammer—A hammer about three feet long with a heavy metal head. It is used to break up rocks.

survivor—Someone who lives through danger or hard times.

synthetics—Materials made by humans that copy materials made by nature.

LEARN MORE

Books

Brown, Cynthia Light. *Amazing Kitchen Chemistry Projects You Can Build Yourself.* White Junction, VT: Nomad Press, 2008.

Casey, Susan. *Kids Inventing!: A Handbook for Young Inventors.* Hoboken, N.J.: John Wiley & Sons, Inc., 2005.

Stewart, Gail B. *Stephanie Kwolek: Kevlar.* Farmington Hills, MI: KidHaven, 2008.

Thimmesh, Catherine. *Girls Think of Everything: Stories of Ingenious Inventions by Women.* Boston: Houghton Mifflin Co., 2000.

Waisman, Charlotte S. *Her Story: A Timeline of the Women Who Changed America.* New York: HarperCollins, 2008.

LEARN MORE

Internet Addresses

If you want to find out more about Stephanie Kwolek, visit these Web sites:

Lemelson Center's Invention at Play: Inventors' Stories—Stephanie Kwolek: Kevlar ™ Inventor
<www.inventionatplay.org/inventors_kwo.html>

The Great Idea Finder: Inventor Stephanie Kwolek
<www.ideafinder.com/history/inventors/kwolek.htm>

If you want to learn more about becoming an inventor, check out these Web sites:

Inventnow.org
<http://www.inventnow.org/>

The Inventive Kids Blog
<http://www.inventivekids.com/>

The U.S. Patent and Trademark Office Kids' Pages
<http://www.uspto.gov/web/offices/ac/ahrpa/opa/kids/index.html>

INDEX